sour cream
and
vinegar

the deplorable poet

~Selected Poems~
"when milk and honey are not enough"

NEWMAN SPRINGS PUBLISHING
320 Broad Street
Red Bank, NJ 07701

First originally published by Newman Springs Publishing 2020

ISBN 978-1-64801-944-9 (Paperback)
ISBN 978-1-64801-945-6 (Hardcover)
ISBN 978-1-64801-946-3 (Digital)

Printed in the United States of America

To Bob and Frazelle Tucker: You were our rock while growing up, and your faith became the foundation.

INTRODUCTION

A note to the reader: I appreciate the time you are taking in reading a sample of my work. I consider myself a confessional imagist poet. I believe in writing in such a way that the reader forms images in their mind while the content is being displayed for them to digest. As a libertarian, I often write on controversial subjects. Often, the subjects are expressed in a way that is not politically correct. I make no apologies for this. We all have different views and beliefs, and it should be a fundamental right of everyone to be able to hold them. After reading my work, regardless of your feelings, it is my hope as a writer that the poetry that I have created will touch you in some way.

—the deplorable poet, Greg Tucker

Uber

So much depends
Upon

Having 5G network
Available

When locating an
Uber

In a bar,
Drunk.

REDEMPTION

Combat
In
My
Head,
In
A
Battle
That
Never
Existed.

Turmoil
Shackles
My
Spirit.

Self-absorption
Is
The
Interrogator
To
My
Existence.

Conflicted
Energy
Soars
Through

My
Veins.

I
Wish
I
Could
Break
Free.

Self-perseverance
Continues
To
Be
The
Leading
Warrior
In
This
Quiddity.

My love
Ones
Drives
Me
To
Be
Better,
Though
The
Judas
Within
Continues
To
Be
The

Villain
In
This
Game.

Maybe
The
Saul
That
Characterizes
Me
Will
One
Day
Evolve
Me
Into
A
Paul,
Where
Redemption
Will
Emerge.

DICK FREE

I am on
A pilgrimage
Of not
Being a dick.

My wife, kids,
Mother, and siblings
Though
Remind
Me
With love
That

I have not
Gotten
To this
Promise land
Yet.

They say
I act
As though
I know
Everything,
While
I interpret
This
Perception

To the fact
That
They first
Knew
Me
When

I understood
Nothing,

Completely
Oblivious
To
The
World
Around
Me.

Now that
I have
Knowledge
And
Experience,
My egotistical
Personality
Wants
The world
To feel it.

Being a dick
Is like
Having
A civil war
Inside
Of me,
Where

The innocent, ignorant
Child
Engages battle
With the intellectual
Scholar
I have
Become.

As I progress
Through this
Journey
To
Enlightenment,

It is my hope
That my love
Ones
Will embrace
The kind child
Still
Within
Me,
While
Accepting
The determined
Warrior
I am.

In the end,
I am beginning
To comprehend
That confidence
And being
A *dick*
Should not

Necessarily
Go hand in hand,
For when
You have
Truly achieved
Confidence,
It is not
Necessary
To show
The
Cards
You
Hold.

Rain Fell Dry

The rain fell
Dry.
Images
Held captive
In the mind
Of a poet,
Whose ink
Lay
Motionless,
Waiting
For the
Medicine
To settle
In.

Soon…

Soothing

Words
Will flow
Through
The fingers,
Seducing
Tranquility
To transpire,

Leaving the
Reader
To partake
In
A
Literary communion,
Allowing
The reader
And author
To become
One
To
Poetic
Prose.

Peace,
Love
Becomes
The editor
And publisher
For the
World to
See.

IF WE COULD BE THERE

Blue skies,
Diversion
To my pain.

Silent
Voices
Scream.

Echoes
Smother
Words
That
Cannot
Be heard.

Hell's
Rain
Black
With toxin,

Designed
To intimidate

The
Senses

Take a step back and think...

If we could
Be there,

You holding
My hand,

Like a toddler
With no
Worry in the
World,
As your strong
Hand
Grasps mine.

If we could be there,

Where green fields
Conquer

A cold steel rail.

A cool breeze
Swallows
Hot air.

An ocean
Replaces
The fish bowl,

Leaving our souls
To scatter
Freely in a
Never-ending
Great deep.

Searching peacefully

For the octopus's garden,
Where
Shelter from
The storm

Becomes
A secret
Hideaway
From
Fear,
Sadness,
Reality,

Knowing you
Still exist
Somewhere,
If not just
In my dreams.

I wish my words
Had came
Out
The last time
We spoke.

Maybe then,
The spirit

Could long
For the
Question
To

If we could be there…

Sour Cream and Vinegar

A Reaction to Milk and Honey

I tried
Reading
Your
Work
With
An
Open
Mind.

Really,
I did.

However,

When
Your
Used
To
Eating
Filet mignon,

It's hard
To

Digest
An instant
Cup of
Noodles
Soup.

I get the
Fact
That
You are
Trying
To
Express
A new
Form
Of
Poetry,

Aren't we all?

The substance
Is

Lacking…

When
I read
The content
Of

Milk and Honey,

Though I have
Been told
It is about
Survival

And
Today's
Feminism,

All I really
Get
From
It

Is a millennial's
Sorry
Attempt
To
Express
Bitterness
In a way
That
The
Author
Receives
Instant
Gratification,
Or a free trophy
From
The
Audience
Of
Instagram.

Sounds

More
Like
SOUR CREAM

AND
VINEGAR

than

MILK AND HONEY

to me.

APATHY

I think
At
Some point,
We live in
A state
Of apathy.

The love
Given
Is quickly
Taken
Away.

I miss you,
I adored
You,
I took
Advantage
Of
The
Love
You
Had.

For
Your
Son,

I have
Regrets.
I feel
Remorse.

I am
In
Mourning,
And
I am
Not
Sure
If
I
Will
Ever
Leave
This

State.

Comforting
Words
Mean
Nothing.

A lot
Of
Despair
Going
On.

I guess
I live
Now
For

My
Offspring.

My example
Though

Will
Never
Equal
What
You
Provided.

Veteran Convict

So much depends
Upon

Robbing a bank
Organized,

Having a clear
Getaway

And not using
Lyft.

SOCIAL DISTANCING

A week
Ago,
They
Preached
Inclusion
Today.
Social
Distancing
Is
The
New
Buzz
Word.

Maybe
The
Term
MYOB (mind your own business)
Could
Be
Utilized
Instead.

Seriously,
The
Government,
Media,
Social networks

Progressive
Asshole
Neighbors.
I think
It is time
For
An
Adult
Time-out.

Stand in the corner.

Breath of Grace

I am
Always
In touch
With
My
Rainbow,
Though
My
Sights
On it
Is
From
A
Dark
Chamber
That
Pain
Provides.

I am
Lost,
Though
I live
As
I am
Found.

"Fake it
Until
You
Make
It"
Is the force
That
Drives
Me.

Awake,
I suppress
The agony
I feel inside.
Asleep,
The demons
Have a free for all,
Releasing
The
Leash
That
Controls
The
Insanity
That
I shamefully
Feel.

Forever fearful
Of abandonment.
I have already
Lost
My dad
Through
Death,
And siblings

Through
My actions
That I did
On my own
Accord.

My offspring
Stays
With
Me.
My spouse
Continues
To hold my
Hand,
And
My mother
Has already
Reached
My
Rainbow
In
Her
Belief
In
Me.

One day,
And one
Day soon,
In life,
Not
Death.
This is
Where
I will
Stand

At the
End
Of God's
Promise,
Where
The shackles
Of
Self-inflicted
Turmoil
Is
Broken
By
The
Breath
Of
Grace.

DOGS RULE

In our home,
Dogs rule.

Don't get
Me
Wrong,
I love
The fuckers.

However,
Mother Hen,
Knowing
The chickadees

(Our grown sons)
Have
Departed
The
Coop,

Has decided
To cope
By
Daunting
Her
Attention
With
These
Mutts.

They eat
Better.
They
Get an
Unlimited
Amount
Of toys,
And
They have
Taken
Over
Our
Bed
At

Night
When I
Sleep.

As far
As
Voicing
My concerns,
I have
Been
Told
I
Better not
Go
There.

What the
Fuck!

I might
As
Well
Retire
Myself
In
The
Dog house
That
They
Never
Use,

Because
In
My
House,
The
Dogs
Rule.

THE BEAST IN ME

The beast in me
Lies
In
Wait,
Salivating
For
A
Score
To
Settle.

The beast in me
Ignores
The
Values
Taught
In Sunday
School
During
My youth.

The beast in me
Wears a leash
Called self-control,
Which is guided
More by self-perseverance
Than moral convictions.

Though
The still small (Holy Spirit)
Voice
Remains
A guide
To what would
Otherwise
Be pure
Self-destruction.

SOCIETY'S
Culture
Has now
Transformed
In the wind.
What was truth
Is now fiction,
And what was
Taboo
Becomes the
Norm.

For a lawman,
Trouble awaits
As the demons
Scatter the
Earth,
Like cockroaches
Attacking
Improper
Storage of
Produce
In a warehouse.
I feel more and
More

Compelled
To unleash
The beast in me.

CORNFIELD OF ABANDONMENT

I think
Hell
Is like
Being
In
A cornfield,
Miles from
Anyone,
ABANDONED.

Prayers
Being
Screamed,
While
Crows
Above
Mocks
The
Echoes
Of
Desperate
Cries.

The soul
Mimicking
A small
Child
Who has

Been left
To wander
In wet
Pants (soiled from urination),
Fearful
To what
Is to
Come.

Yes,
I think
Hell
Is an infinite
Cornfield,
Where
Communication
To our
Creator
And the
Ones we
Love
Ceases.

Sometimes,
This poet
Feels
As though
Hell
Is already
Present.

GRIEF

10.06.2018 14:41

Grief
Is when
Epiphany
Makes
You
Aware
That
Communication
Is
No
Longer
Accessible
To

A love
One
Who
Has passed
Away.

Grief
Becomes
A predator
To dreams
And
A
Tormentor
When
You
Awake.

Grief
Is not
Subdued
By
Condolence,
Nor
Does
It
Fade
By keeping
Busy.

In the
End,
Grief
Is a persistent
Virus
That spreads
From

The
Mind
To
The soul,
And eventually
Invades
The
Spirit.

Grief
Tells
Us
That life
Is not
Infinite.
It is cruel,
And
Hope
Is just
An
Illusion
That is
Used
As snake oil
To make
Us believe
That there
Is
Meaning
To
Living.

Stained Hourglass

The hourglass
To my soul
Is stained
As though
It should
Be displayed
As one of the
Windows
At
Sainte Chappelle
Cathedral.

Stories,
Emotions
Drawn
And
Shaped
With painfully
Detailed
Artistic
Expression.

Each character
Upon
It
Has a
Vibrant
Living
Energy.

My hourglass
Is
A
Day,
A
Life
Into
This
Poet's
Spirit.

Friends
And lovers
Who
Have
Came
And
Gone
Serve
As
Sweet
And
Bitter
Memories
Of who
I am.

Though
My hourglass
Has
An
Expiration
Date,
The sand
That
Flows
Through
It
Is
Eternal.

For it is
A representation
Of a godlike image,
Infinite
As the universe
That
Surrounds
It.

Existing but Not Living

I exist
But
I have stopped
Living.

I dream,
Yet
There
Is no
Hope.

I pray,
Though
The
Words
Seem
To
Go
Nowhere.

Empty
Promises;
Optimism
Gone
Array.

Just an
Overimaginative
Boy,
Persuading
His
Younger
Sister
That there
Is treasure
Underneath
The neighbor's
Rose garden.

Forty-six years later,
And many whippings
from my folks.

I still cannot help
To believe
That
Somewhere
There must
Be treasure,
Or
Lucky
Numbers
On the
Lottery tickets
I POSSESS.

Morning Slumber

Where
The spirit
And the
Now meet
Is during
The morning
Slumber,
A time
Of refuge,
A safe
Haven,
The unspoken
Temple.

Inner
Conflict
Resolution
Becomes
The topic
Between
The soul
And spirit,
Allowing
Healing
And
Cognitive
Objectives
To be
The advocates
To rejuvenation.

The morning
Slumber
Takes
The
Despair
Of a kamikaze
And
Reincarnates
It
Into
A Self-preserving
Messiah,

Leaving
The dawn
To
Be the
Candlelight
That

Is
Resilient
To
Wind.

EPSTEIN

A broken neck,
Lost
Video coverage,
Ignoring
Logical
Reasoning,
And lack of
Media
Interest
Gives
Rise
To
What
Stares
In front
Of the
Viewer,
A rabid
Dog
Called
Corruption.

The
Pocket
Watch
Continues
To move
As a distraction.

The public
Is left in
A trance.

Zombies
To a
October-like
Revolution,
Disarming
The lambs
For
Slaughter.

Ethics,
Morality
Is for
The weak
And impoverished,
While gluttony
And depravity
Are
Bounties
For the
1 percent.

Media
Manufactured
Truth,
Creates
Headlines,
Conspiring

To rob
Our
Youth
Of democracy.

Licking You

My doggy
Mouth
Cannot
Quite
Make
A kiss,
So I licked
You
Straight
On the lips.

You were
Sleeping
On the couch,
Reminded
Me
Of
A
Human
Angel,

So I licked
You.

I am
Sorry
If I startled
You,
Just wanted
To show
You
Some affection.

I think
You are
My
Best
Friend,
So
I licked
You.

DAMN IT, JOE

Damn it, Joe,
Have you
Ever
Heard of
Personal spaces?

I know your
Boy
Likes
The powder,
And you're
Trying
To get
On my
Good side,
But

I am feeling
Uncomfortable.

THE INK OF ENLIGHTENMENT

I kiss
The ink
As it creates
The literary
Sky.

Imagery
Molded
As pillow,
Like
Clouds
Fills
Your imagination.

Dreams
Are invaded
As my conscious
Mind
Whispers
To your
Subconscious.

Like a
Delightful
Culinary
Presentation,
A poet's
Words

Sparks
The
Reader's
Appetite.

Hopefully,
The seduction
Breeds
A craving
That
Drives
The audience
To wanting
More.

Relax,
Breathe
Softly,
I am
In
Your
Mind
Now.

Let
The
Words
Flow
Through
You
Like
A river
Of
Tranquility,
Swiftly
Carrying

You
To
The
Shore
Of
Enlightenment.

The Devil's Advocate

Spoke to
The devil
Today.
You were
The main
Subject
Of conversation.

In light of
Attorney's
Client
Privilege,
The content
Cannot
Be disclosed,
But let's
Just
Say
Things
Are not
Looking
Good
For
You.

Your
Lukewarm
Defense

That
You
Are devising
Is going to be spit
Out
By the court
As you
Were forewarned
To go either
Hot or cold.

Next time,
Listen
To the revelations
That are
Handed to
You.

Being accused
Of breaching
A contract
Is never
Restful;
However,
When
The plaintiff
Buys
A verdict
With thirty pieces
Of silver
From a jury
Of your
Peers,

I can imagine
There
Can be
A little
Bit
Of
Stress
Going
On,

Not to mention
That the
Judgment
Of your
Soul
Is
What
Will
Ultimately
Be
What is
Rewarded.

My advice?

Settle!

Red-Eye Cauldron

I feel as
Though
A marker
Has been
Placed
On
Me,
Like the
Curse
Of
Caine,
A Stench
That cannot
Be
Removed.

I taunted
The bees
Of elysian.
Their honey
Became
A scorching,
Like
Cyanide
Burning
Holes
Within
My

Breath,
Injecting
Toxics
Within
My
Veins,
Turning
A tornado
Like virus
To batter
My
Soul.
My spirit
Is
Not
Whole.

Using
Muscle
Memory
I systematically
Forced.
My
Nerves
To
Calm
And
Wait
For that
Still
Small
Voice
To guide
Me to
The

Meadow
Of tranquility.

With
Chaos
And
Disruption
Comes
A
Reincarnation
Of
Peace.

I know
My pathway
Will once
Again
Become
Easy.
Mana
Will
Come
To
Me
With
The
Red-eye
Cauldron
Of dawn.
The birds
Will
Sing
A
New
Day,

And yesterday's
Trouble
An
Afterthought.

Happy Father's Day

I have lost
Friends
Over the years.
I have experienced
Pain
Greater than
The
Average
Joe,
But
Losing
You,
Dad,

Is
Something
I
Could
Never
Prepare
For.

I wanted
To
Say
The
Final
Goodbye,
But
Time
Stole
This
From
Me.

Whispers
In
The
Wind
Tell
Me
That
Your
Energy
Remains
Vibrant
And
Alive,
Though
The

Distance
Cannot
Be measured
As
It formulates
From
Another
Dimension.

My dreams,
My memories,
My subconscious
Extends
My spiritual
Hand,
Hoping
For
Just
A
Brief
Connection
So
That
The
Soul
May find
Solace,
Knowing
It is
More
Than
Dust
To
Dust.

Yes, I have
Felt
Pain
Before,
Yet
In this
Instance,
Life
Has
Breathed
Its poisonous
Breath
To
Remind
Me
That death
Will
Not
Discriminate,
And
The fatherly
Love
That
I have known
A lifetime
Is permanently
Taken
In this
Existence.

No fillers
Are available,
No
Words
Of
Comfort

Will
Satisfy
This
Void,
Just
A gnawing
Reminder
That there
Will
Be
More
To
Come.

Selfishly,
I hope
I am
Next.

INTO MY INK

Into her breath,
I invaded
Her emotions.

Into my soul,
Her thoughts
Enslaved me.

Into her
Routines,
I became
A priority.

Into my
My muscle
Memory,
I carried on
Because of
Her.

Into her
Dreams,
I was made
The heroic
Character.

Into my ink,
She became
My talent,
My imagery,
My eternal
Muse.

Into us,
We
Are
One.

Informant

My knees
failed me

As I took
that *motherfucker*
Down.

Hand restraints
Placed on
With a twist,

Showing colors
No longer
Seemed
Meaningful
As
He became
A gang
Of
One,

Turned
Informant
For
Self-preservation.

The rules
Do not
Apply
When
Your
Facing
Time.

CALLING IN SICK

I get
The fact
That time
To time,
One must
Call in sick,

And

You may
Not
Even be
Sick.

This
Is okay.
Not everyone
Has a good
Work
Ethic.

However,
If you're one
Of those
Who does
It several
Times

A
Year,

Though
Your
Boss
And
Coworkers
Won't
Say
It,
I will say,

"You're a loser!"

WAITING FOR ORDERS

I have come
To realize
That I
Have been
Waiting
For orders
Since 1994
In the
Fox hole
Of my soul.

My current
Grid,
"Lima, Lima, Mike Foxtrot."

This soldier
Has yet
To
Fulfill
His
Patriotic
Duty.

So in
Transit,
I await.

Fallen soldiers
Are not
Always,
In the
Physical
Sense,
Dead.

Sometimes,
We are
Trapped
In a
Mental
Purgatory
Post,
In which
We have
Yet
To of
Been
Relieved
Of
Duty.

For me,
Though
Life
Has brought
Me
Joy,
Sorrow,
And the
Greatest
Family
A man
Could

Have,
I still
Wait
To complete
The
Assignment
That I am
Called
To
Do.

In silence,
I vehemently
Await
Destiny.

Jesus Unfriended Me

I believe
Jesus
Has
Unfriended
Me
As I
Feel
As though
I am
In a
Soundproof
Studio
Room,
Where
My prayers
And pleas
Cannot
Get out.

Maybe
God
Is just
Telling
Me that
I made
My bed,
And now

I just need to
Lie in it.

IDK...

At
This
Point
In
My
Life,
I am
Asking
For
An
Olive
Branch,
Just
One card
Played
In my
Favor.

I realize
Though,
Because
Of my
Screwups,
You may
Want
To have
Control
Of the whole
Hand,
And
I am cool

With that.
You can
Take my
Place at
The table
If
You
Want.

Some Men

Some Men
Don't belong
Walking the
Earth,
For
Depravity
Has
Infected
The lifeline
Of their
Souls.

No
Treatment,
No cure,
No sentence
Of purgatory
Will cleanse
Their spirit,
Just an
Eternal
Journey
To damnation
Is the redemption
For mankind.

Liberal created
Appeals,

Inmate services
And
Programs
Designed
To humanize.
The monsters
Are the continued
Daggers of
Evil
Placed on the
Victims,
When
Quick
Finality
Would serve
A better
Course.

Some men
Don't belong
Walking
The
Earth,
And
Our empathy
Should
Be removed
At their
Extraction.

Did I Forget You?

Did I forget
You
While I
Sprayed
My Ink
Across
The web?

Did I ignore
You
While formulating
Words within
My head?

Being egocentric
And sometimes
Ethnocentric
Tends to be
Traits of
A writer.
Our intellectual
Snobbery
Also often
Gets in the way.

For after all,
The poet
Writes about

The world that
He or she sees,
The emotions felt,
And the perception
that
One has of the people
Interacting in the small
Dwelling
He or she
Inhabits.

By nature,
The script that
One writes
Is
One-sided.
From a narcissist
Who believes
What he or she
Has to
Say is
Somehow
Unique
And incredible
Upon
Its
Birth,

And yet,

It is the audience's
Response and
Emotions to
What we
Write
That fuels

The creativity
That drives
The pen.

I guess it is
A catch-22,
To be frank
About it.

In one hand,
I genuinely
Adore
And respect
When a reader
Relates and feel
The emotions
Into what I
Write.

On the other hand,
If the reader
Doesn't try
To relate
Or
Is more interested
In reading poems
WITH PICTURES,
Then I am okay
In writing to
The audience
OF
ME
MYSELF
AND
I.
At least

Then, I
Know
The
Spectator
Can
Absorb
At least
10 percent
Of
What
I *am*
Trying
To
Convey.

ARIEL'S FINAL JOURNEY
TRIBUTE TO SYLVIA

Before the red-eye
Cauldron of morning,
While
Dark-eye
Berries
Cast their
Hooks
And black-sweet blood,
Mouthful Shadows
Surround me,
I soar
As an arrow
Into the stasis
Of the night.
Epiphany's messenger
Summons me,
Declaring that my
Poetic equestrian
Excursion
Has abruptly
Halted to an end.

In hindsight,
My life has
Been ridden
Like "Lady Godiva,"

Bareback,
Naked,
Exposing
My mortal deformities
For the literary world
To see.

Lack of Daddy's
Presence
Has created
A leak
Within this
Vessel,
Preventing
Any joy
Or happiness
To permanently
Keep.
Electroconvulsive
Therapy
Was ordered
To harness
My demons.
The outcome
Though
Has crippled
My physical well-being
And suppressed
My creative expression.
The latter, I am
Unable to
Concede
To.
Therefore, it
Is time for
This pen

To retire
And the terminal
Narrative to end.
My oven's
Gas chambers
Hearkens me,
Beckoning
To enter it's
Domain.
Maybe then,
Within
It's
Warm
Embrace,
I will
Find
Eternal peace.

A Bridge to Nowhere

It is time
to cross.

Volumes
Of memories

Will go
with you.
Your thoughts,
Your secrets,

Kept under
Lock, and
Key
In the
Inner vault
Of your
Soul.

Sins
Of yesterday,
Regrets
For today,
And nightmares
Of tomorrow
Are the vessels
That provide
Passage

Through
The bridge
Of nowhere.

A dark place,
Where kites
Of prayers
Are left
Crumbled,
Alongside a prison's
Corridor,
Acting
As tickets
To gain admission
To the bridge
To nowhere.

No turning
Back,
No apologies,
Dramatic
Imprints
On an
Egocentric
Pandora's
Box
Leads the
Way
To
A moment of
Personal
Intervention,
ACCEPTANCE,
And one last
Adrenaline rush
Before the

Acknowledgment
That
There
Is a bridge to
Nowhere.

LISTENING WITH YOUR EYES

Most people
Listen 5 percent
Of the time,
When they
Should be
Listening
90 percent,
While trying
To find resolution
To a conflict.

Next time,
When you
Engage
In conversation
With a stranger,
Take the time
To notice
The color
Of their eyes.

By doing so,
You open
Your tunnel
Vision,
Where your
Eyes become
Your ears

And the truth
Becomes
Apparent
To
What was
Not said.

I call this
The Tucker Effect.

THE FOX AND THE BLACKBIRD

Years of oppression,
The mother hen
To society's
Unwanted.
The Blackbird
Sings a lullaby,
Nestled in an old
Barn,
Deep within
The plantation.

Hungry for power,
Enticed by
Her vulnerability,
The red Fox
Devises a way
To feed upon
The Blackbird's
Economic distress.

Invitations
To free housing,
Free education,
Free food,
And free
Transportation
To see her
Chicks

Held unjustly
In the state Penn,
The red Fox
Manipulates
The Blackbird
In entering into
A contract
To stick it
To the man.

Without reading
The small details,
The Blackbird
Became blindly
Indebted,
And
Promises of freedom
Were replaced
By political slavery.
Confidence evolved
Into self-doubt
And dependency.

Oppression had
No chance of
Being lifted
As the Fox
Constantly
Reminded
The bird
Of the man
Seducing
Her to bow
to his command.

Sadly, in the end,
The difference
Between "the Man"
And "the red Fox"
Became indistinguishable
As both
Are predators
Within the game,
Just bourgeoisie
Masters
With
Different
Names.

Blackbird singing in the dead of night,
Take these broken wings and learn to fly.
All your life
You were only waiting for this moment to arise.
You were only waiting for this moment to arise.
You were only waiting for this moment to arise.

Do not submit, Blackbird,
It is your time
To fly.

SHE COMES IN COLORS

She comes in colors
In the fabric
That makes up my
Soul.

A messiah
Of sorts
To the lost
Wolf,
An outcast
To social norms.

Wind
Danced
To her beautiful
Curly hair
The moment
We met.
A soviet
Plunder
To a Jerusalem-inherited
Artifact.

She takes my
Breath away,
And her soft
Voice
Is like no
Other.

Never really
Believed
That there
Was a caretaker
Of a soul
Until
Our paths
Collided.
Then I knew
That God's hope
Often comes in a
Physical manifestation.

The world lately
Has wrapped its
Dark hands
Upon our
Life,
Family,
And existence,
But I live
Today because
She is

The light
Within
This
Black
Tunnel.

THE CLOAK OF DAWN

The cloak of dawn
Is where
Reality is seen
As it is.

With a touch
Of hope placed
In the middle,

Its shield
Protects
Against
The negativity

That often
Serves
As a predator
To our sanity.

The cloth it is
Made of
Is the endless
Possibilities
That our hand
Of creation
Is able
To produce.

There is a reason
Why nature
Sits in quietness
Before
The birth of a new day
Begins.

For Darwinism
Is at full
Force
When the sun rises
And the mantle
Unfolds,
Sparking
Realism
To the incendiary
Of
Self-preservation,
Leaving us
Another day
To conquer
The demons

That our mind
Had generated
From the previous
Night.

CONTAINING THE UNIVERSE

An endless cup
Contains a finite
Amount of rain
As words
Trickle
At the outskirts
Of the universe.

Rivers of joy
And ripples of sorrow
Stream through
My uninhibited
Mind,
Releasing and unminding
Me.
Om Deva Guru Jai.
Everything is going to influence your world.
Everything is going to influence your world.
Everything is going to influence your world.
Everything is going to influence your world.

Depictions of unsevered luminescence, which
Whirled before me like a million peepers.
They beckon me on and on
To the other side of the universe.
Thoughts zigzagged like an
Uneasy breeze inside a pillar box.

They topple over unseeingly
As they make their way across the universe.

Om Deva Guru Jai.
Everything is going to influence your world.
Everything is going to influence your world.
Everything is going to influence your world.
Everything is going to influence your world.

Sounds of viability, shades of chuckling
Are booming through my opened ears,
Seducing and luring me.
Unending infinite adoration, which
Glows around me like a million stars,
Beckons me on and on throughout the universe.

Om Deva Guru Jai.
Everything is going to influence your world.
Everything is going to influence your world.
Everything is going to influence your world.
Everything is going to influence your world.

December 8, 1980,
As bullets traveled

outside *The Dakota,*

The comparison
To Jesus became
More palatable
As you transcended
Into
Omnipotence,
Making your way
On the outskirts of the universe.
Om Deva Guru Jai.

Everything is going to influence your world.
Everything is going to influence your world.
Everything is going to influence your world.
Everything is going to influence your world.

OAK TREE CONCERTO

In light of said events,
I am the mirror to your reflection,
Like lingonberry seeds
Screaming to dance
To the moonlight
Of a midsummer night's
Dream,
So is the awaken contemplation
Of regret.

Acid reflux
Invades slumber
as Hamlet's ghost
Acts as a conductor
To the symphony
Of apathy.

The strings of sorrow
Drowns out the
Flute of joy,
Haunting the performance
Of this motionless soul
On a repetitious soundtrack.

In retrospect,
Climbing up
Too close to GOD
Only caused

The trees to shake,
Thus raining
Acorns of melancholy
Upon this concerto.

It is the hope though,
That since
The composer is
The "Trinity of Forgiveness,"
A kernel of this
Fragmented residue
Will take root,
Forming a
Fortress of *oak*
called "redemption."

Cataracts of the Forbidden Fruit

When Adam
And Eve
Ate the
Forbidden
Fruit,
I believe
It dissolved
The cataracts
Of our
Innocence,
The inability
To accept
Those
Who are
Different
Than us.

The fruit
Became
The serum
Of hate.

The color
Of skin
Became
A sense

Of either
Superiority
Or inferiority.

Religion
Was born,
A tool
Used
To control
Others
As to how
They see
God.

Social classes
Were created,
Where the
Weak
Became weaker,
And those
With means
Oppressed
The poor
By
Either exerting
Their power
Or by
Giving
Out crumbs
To form
Dependency.

Today,
We are
In such
A state

Where
No human
Heart
Has not
Been
Tainted
With
Some
Level
Of hate.

We cannot
Deny it
By owning
Our "privilege"
Because
We are white,
Or say
We are
Exempt
Because
We are black,
Because
The virus
Still dwells
Within.

Our only
Hope
Is that
Society
Will somehow
Begin
To see
The world
Once again

With
Cataracts,
And that
The age
Of innocence
Will
Become
The desired
Place
To be.

LIBERTARIAN POET

This writer
Believes
That everyone
Should have
The right
To live their
Life in peace,
As long as
They are not
Causing harm
To another.

Who you sleep
With should not
Matter.
What you believe,
Or if you even
Believe in a higher
Being at
All,
You should have this
Right
Without fear
Of persecution.

What a woman
Does with
Her body

Should
Not be
Regulated
By
The government,
Nor should
A Baker
Be told
Who
He can
Bake a
Cake for.

The individual's
Right should
Be protected.

America
Is not the
World police.
Unfortunately,
We have, for centuries,
Bought into the
Propaganda by
The government
That somehow
We are
The world's
Hero,
And everything
We do is
For the
Good of
Humanity.

There is a darkness
And sin
That we, as a nation, bare
That we
Have
Not been able
Come to
Terms
With.

A good
Start though
Would
Be restricting
Our global influence
And
Concentrating
With the problems
At home.

Welfare,
Obamacare,
And Obama phones
Are all
Examples
Of
Metaphorical whips
Used
By the government
That are
Designed
To keep
The slave
In line.

Charity,
Churches,
And Community
Groups should
Lead the way
To help
Those
Who cannot
Help
Themselves,
Not the government.

Wake Up!
There is no such
Thing as a free
Ride
When it comes
From big brother.

Food stamps
Create
Dependency,
Which
Leads
To the depletion
Of self-worth
And dignity.

This poet
Loves America
And is a veteran,
Patriot, and God-fearing
Citizen,
But in light

Of the power struggles
With the ruling
Parties,
Someone needs to speak
Up
And say,
"This pond
Is not
Safe to
Drink
From
As
Political
Greed
Has
Contaminated
Its water
And compromised
Its
Integrity!"

Let's find
A better
Way
By reducing
The powers
Of an intrusive
Government
And
Become
"We the people"
Again.

After all,
Are we not
The home of the brave?

I Am Woman (Ode to Poetess Ann Sexton)

You once said:

"Put your ear down close to your soul and listen hard,"

Yet most of us never listen.

Confessional poet
Feminist to the time,
Inspiration
to the novice,
Seductive
In verse,
You were
All, woman.

As it drills
Into the
Marrow
Of your
Bone,

Dream
Lacking
GPS,
The street
Called

"Mercy"
Was never
Found.

Maybe this
Is why
Apathy
Settled
In
As the
Car engine
Ran
Within
The confines
Of your
Sealed
Garage.

The reciprocator
Of
Mercilessness
Procreates
Hopelessness.

Did intellect
Come to you
To the point
That you
Knew
So much
Yet you
Knew nothing?

Was this
The
Splinter

That
Cracked
The sparrow's
Neck?

Within the resting
Grounds
Of poets
Lie
Much
Unfinished
Life,
Unfinished
Ink.

Victims
Of their
Own
Creativity,
Which served
As the
Engineer
To their
Dissolution.

You Have
Ridden in
The cart,
Last bright
Routes
Survivor,
And as the
Flames
Bit your
Thigh,
You stood

Proudly
As a woman
Not afraid to
Die.

POE'S ROOMMATE TELLS ALL

I am not at all
Concerned.
If you think
I am mad,
In contrast,
I find it
Rather amusing.

Seriously,
Like you,
The
Reader,
Would somehow

Qualify as
An
Expert
Or authority
To
Diagnose
My mental
Well-being.

I am only
Writing this,
Which I will call
The unabridged version
Of *The Tell-Tale Heart*,
To set the matter straight.

You see, a few years ago,
I was sharing a room
At the institution
With quite an
Annoying writer
Named Edgar.

One uneventful night,
I was sitting on
My bunk
Listening to
Edgar,
Who apparently
Was having
A psychotic
Episode
By
Trying to mimic
A bird
Squawking

The words
"Nevermore"
As he vigorously
Scribbled ink
Upon his desk.

To shut him up,
I proceeded
To tell him
The crime
I was convicted
Of
Concerning
The old man.

Much to my dismay,
The "Father of Horror"
Later
Took it upon himself
To plagiarize the
Tale (writing in first person),
Distort the events,
And unfairly portray
Me as a madman
With a conscience.

For the record,
I am neither mad,
Nor do I have
A conscience,
Just a "law-abiding citizen,"
Who got tired of having
To live with a dude
With a "vulture eye."

It is not like

I did not forewarn
The geezer.

On numerous
Occasions,
I told him
To cover
That shit up
With some *Raybans*
Or a patch,
But
The bastard did not
Listen,
So I bashed his
Head in,

Dismembered
Him,
And placed
The pieces of
His body
Under the planks
Of my floor.

As far as the sound of the
Beating heart
Goes,
It turns out
The old man's
Amazon, Alexa,
Was sarcastically
Playing
Hilary Duff's
"Beat of My Heart"
In the background
To set *the mood*.

I informed the
Piece of tin
To knock that crap
Off, or meet
The same demise
As her master.

Quite surprisingly,
In a fearful breath,
She complied.

Today, as fate would have it,
I am being released.

To appease my
"Tell-tale heart
And newfound conscience,"
I will be looking up
An old dear friend
Who I was told
Can be seen
Staggering along
The cobble streets
Of Baltimore.

It is then I will
Silence forever
The "squawks of nevermore."

WASHED IN THE BLOOD

I know
Regardless
Of life's
Circumstances,

I am washed in
The blood of
The lamb.

I know it is
Nothing
I have
Done,
Or am doing
To deserve
This

As his gift was
Free to accept,
And
Therefore,
I am washed in

The blood of
The lamb.

Today,
I feel

The tide
Coming
In
So much,
So
I feel
As though
I am drowning,
Yet
I find
Solace
In knowing
That
I am washed
In the
Blood of the lamb.

In peace,
I wait
For
Tranquility
To
Stomp
Out life's
Anarchy,
Knowing
I am washed
In the
Blood of the lamb.

THAT KISS

A kiss
Can mean
A lot.
It can
Be affection,
Respect,
Love,
Fear,
Sympathy,
Or
In
Recognition
Of betrayal.

I believe
The significance
Of a kiss
Is seen
As a symbol
Of a connection
Between
Two,

Where emotions
Merge
With our
Humanity.

THE IMMORTALITY OF A WRITER

The aroma
Of a full-bodied Cuban
Fills the senses
As pellets spray across the atmosphere.
The feline community will soon mourn your passing.

Old man,
The sea continues to beckon you
With the conclusion of every sunset.
Does the narcissistic verse of Plath and Sexton
Aggravate you?
Or are they just simple companions
To the fields of elysian?

Talent is not taken.
It is only the vessel
That was left lifeless
Within the cobble streets
Of Baltimore.

For upon the tell-tale heart
Of every reader,
The raven continues
To chant,
And the absence of plums
Are still vacant
In the ice box,
Though the critic

Still questions the
Merit of its validity.

My friend,
Songs will continue to be written
About her
As she is the representation
That innocence
Will always be contaminated
By the conflict
Between
Reasoning and emotions,
Leaving the bird's squawks
Of "nevermore"
Forever ignored.

ABOUT THE AUTHOR

the deplorable poet (Greg A. Tucker) is a modern-day confessional imagist. He holds two master degrees in criminal justice (criminology), legal studies and currently working on his third master degree in forensic behavioral science (victimology). Being a true libertarian at heart, the deplorable poet's views on an individual's God-given right to make their own choices in life, which sometimes includes not being "politically correct," is often depicted in the ink that he produces. He also attempts to bring a mixture of humor, sorrow, and hope to those who take the time to read his work, allowing them a chance to relate to the journey that all humans take called "life."

www.thedeplorablepoet.org

CPSIA information can be obtained
at www.ICGtesting.com
Printed in the USA
BVHW071338131221
623915BV00001B/8